Just Cooking

Bart De Pooter, Just Cooking

With texts by Willem Asaert and photography by Bart Van Leuven, published by ɫ lannoo

Flanders is one of the most prosperous regions in Europe, with a richly chequered cultural life. Literature, art, theatre, music and design, fashion and gastronomy all reach outstanding heights internationally.

One of the culinary standard-bearers is Bart De Pooter. Just south of the town and world port of Antwerp is his restaurant Pastorale, a former presbytery with a contemporary interior. Here he offers a personal and refreshing cuisine which is consistently extremely well-thought-out and at the same time very accessible.

As an alternative to world trends, such as fast food, fusion and molecular gastronomy, the emphasis in Pastorale is on the quality of the Flemish culinary heritage which its owner brings up to date as a permanent 'work in progress'. In the kitchen the staff uses the most modern techniques and the chefs by preference use regional and ecological products combined with products from sustainable agriculture.

Bart De Pooter's compositions are based on logic and emotion or perfectly mastered techniques and intense taste perceptions. In his scintillating dishes he gives plenty of room to mildly sour and bitter touches, which, as in the finest wines, add character and excitement.

With an unbelievable depth of taste, attention for the feel in the mouth, and coquettish, feminine accents, he adds a playful nervousness to his light and fluid dishes which lingers and at the same time bestows a fascinating, captivating and personal experience.

Pastorale: Past, Oral, and Emotions

Starting from the past, we create oral and other sensory sensations based on emotions.
Our story is told with these emotions.

Respect for the Past

Chef Bart De Pooter and his wife and hostess Marie-Claire see themselves as temporary caretakers of an exceptional building. From the start the couple wanted to show respect for the former presbytery, which – because of its historic architectural significance – is a listed building. The house, of which the plans date back to 1836-1837, lies on the edge of the town centre of Reet and served as a presbytery until the 1980s. It is a textbook example of a late classicist nineteenth-century presbytery, and consists of a two-storey, symmetrical, double-fronted house under a slate roof. By the end of the twentieth century the building showed signs of serious deterioration as a result of poor maintenance. The high cost of restoration persuaded the local council, who owned it, to put the building and part of the garden into the hands of property developers. As a result, the presbytery was restored in 1991 and renamed the 'Restaurant Pastorale'.

Refurbishing philosophy

When in 1992 the tenancy of the building came into the hands of chef Bart De Pooter and his wife Marie-Claire Braem, it very quickly experienced a 'revival'. The couple first of all carried out a thorough historical study of the building, which revealed that on the site of the presbytery there had once been a comparable medieval, and later a renaissance residence of which the earliest mention goes back to 1575. The parish of Reet itself was founded in 1308. The efforts of the present-day tenants have gradually revived the site. In 1995 the building underwent a thorough renovation, concentrating on the exterior. Nine years later followed a second campaign of restoration to restore the interior. In this a refurbishing philosophy was followed that showed respect for the building as a monument and at the same time focused on the comfortable and efficient reception of their guests. The integration of contemporary art contributes in such a way that the serene and contemplative spirit of the place, the genius loci, is enhanced. In this way the temporary caretakers of the building are reconciling the past with the present.

A work in progress

In this way the total concept became a 'work in progress' which hides behind the Pastorale, both in the material and the spiritual sense. 'I see "Pastorale" as a brand, which in fact I registered as such some ten years ago. Every brand has a specific concept, and within that concept you have a number of levels. In the first place we are operating in a classic building dating from 1837, which we treat with respect, but still give a real contemporary atmosphere and feel. In that building we are running a 'work in progress' project with, among other things, a continuous process of evolution in the kitchen, where there is plenty of scope for new techniques to present lighter, healthier, more tasteful and yet recognizable dishes. Here our ambition is to offer tomorrow's classics too. In addition we have given the space round the building, and more specifically the garden which has gradually gained in importance, a formal role. To gauge our ideas on this, we have started working with designers who have also guided us in internal arrangements in the building. Our ultimate aim is that everything should blend harmoniously together.

There are, for instance, paintings here based on mayonnaise, and the mantelpiece on the first floor is painted on a base of rabbit skin from which glue was made. It sounds very avant-garde, but it is actually just an environmentally-friendly painting technique of 1730. Besides this we have enriched the restaurant with contemporary art. Not only for a purely aesthetic effect, but also because these plastic works inspire us, and hopefully also our guests. It is in that light, for example, that you should look at a fragment from Virgil, which enriches one of our ceilings. Everything is designed to give our guests a feeling of pleasure and enrichment. Naturally the base is always our kitchen, where superior products are the starting point for pampering our guests, and in which new techniques are only applied to bring new sensations to the plate, and to give considered form to new and special taste impressions.'

KOM HIERHEEN, SCHONE JONGELING,

LELIES BRENGEN DE NIMFEN JE,

KIJK, KORVEN VOL.

STRALEND PLUKT VOOR JOU DE NAJADE

BLEEKBLAUWE VIOLEN

EN DE KOP VAN PAPAVERS,

COMBINEERT NARCIS

MET DE BLOEM VAN WELGEURENDE DILLE.

DAN SCHIKT ZE LAVENDEL

EN ANDERE WELDADIGE   KRUIDEN

EN SIERT MET HET GELE   VAN DE GOU-

DERE HYACINTHEN.

ZELF ZOEK IK ZILVERGRIJZE APPELS

BEDEKT MET ZACHTDONZIGE WAAS,

EN KASTANJES WAARVAN MIJN AMARYLLIS ZOVEEL HIE

IK DOE ER WASGELE PRUIMEN BIJ (…),

OOK EEN VLEUGJE ZOUT,

(…)EN JULLIE, LAUWERTAKKEN, PLUK IK AF,

EN JOU OOK, MIRTE ERNAAST

Our own identity

'In this way I have designed a personal cuisine, and one with its own identity based on finished presentations and well-considered taste associations, I have also dared to go beyond the usual lines. For that I can rely on a strong team who are convinced by our business philosophy. Together we hold to the idea of creating food sensations. The desire to stimulate all the senses and to arouse emotions is the incubator of our cuisine. Out of respect for nature we also prefer to go to work as ecologically as possible. We promote the use of sun-ripened products and fish caught by rod and line, and we work by preference with animals traditionally and humanely reared and fed. We also take account of nutritional values and make judicious use of various sugars and fats. The main accent lies on natural flavours. For a healthy and easily digestible cuisine all kinds of techniques are available today, and to apply them correctly is another challenge. What is central to this, and always remains essential in our kitchen, is our continual process towards improvement. Anyone cooking for guests should be continuously critical of themselves. To rest on our laurels in this business and at this level is just not on. I gladly put my cuisine to the question and am always searching for new, small and surprising details to keep my guests happy. I sometimes compare a restaurant with a baroque garden, as a typical place of illusion, surprise and variety, where, on your next visit, you not only want to be entertained, but also surprised. With our dishes we not only want to keep our own spirits high, but also stimulate those of our guests. Guests who taste with enjoyment, look at each other and discuss what they are eating, taste again, discover and start a conversation about their experience, give our team every day anew the necessary drive to achieve our object.'

A world full of fantasy

Like many children Bart de Pooter spent his early years in a world full of fantasy. Fascinated by the magic potions of Merlin the Enchanter, he soon began to take an interest in his mother's daily kitchen preoccupations. And by the time he was ten it was through mere child's play that he began to understand that baking pancakes was more realistic than brewing magic potions. 'In my young teens it became clear that I wasn't really much of a linguist, and so when I was fifteen I went to a hotel school to learn a trade.'
He soon realized that the pocket money he earned as a waiter during weekends was very useful to acquire some culinary experience. With his hard-earned money he visited a starred restaurant for the first time. Impressed by this experience he decided to make an extra effort and at the age of nineteen became a 'commis' in the kitchen of the three-star restaurant Romeyer in Hoeilaart. Within this highly reputable kitchen brigade he was made responsible for fish dishes less than six months later. Shortly after this he was chosen as best Belgian junior chef in a national competition, and a future in the kitchen beckoned. 'If I hadn't become a chef, then I would now probably be a photographer or a designer.' In his early twenties he took on the Pastorale restaurant and in 2003 he earned his first Michelin star. Three years later a second star followed and so, at the age of 38, he became the youngest two-star chef in Belgium. 'A fantastic recognition, which has pleased everyone in Pastorale enormously. But the best part of this trade is the moment when I see the gleam in the eyes of our guests, every time they visibly enjoy one of our dishes.'

Location: 51° 06' N 04° 24' E

Reet is a village in the province of Antwerp. It lies on the Antwerp-Mechelen axis and with Terhagen makes up the municipality of Rumst. Although Reet has the largest area, the largest number of residents and the municipal offices, Rumst is the official municipality. Reet lies in the centre of an extensive area of clay pits which provided plenty of employment up to the 1960s. The clay was scraped out to make bricks, for which the whole Rupel region was famous. Currently there is only one brickworks still working in Rumst.

Photos on previous pages:
Clay pit in Rumst, 2008 (left)
and puffed Bomba di Riso with natural ink, 2008 (right)

Structure and symbiosis of dishes

Starting from a Burgundian tradition, Pastorale strives to produce sensations while eating, and to make a basic necessity into an experience by stimulating all senses. For this we use by preference ecologically responsible products, and we choose kitchen techniques which bring out the authentic pure taste of the ingredients at their best, guarantee their nutritive value, and limit the use of sugars and fats. The object is to create healthy, light, digestible dishes which please all the senses and hone the mind. In this the use of various products from the same natural source leads to harmony on the plate. This means that products that are sown, born or raised in the same environment share a common, harmonious taste. An example of this is the preparation of a Belgian farm chicken in which the use of maize, sunflower seed, barley and buckwheat raised on the same soil, harmonize perfectly. Gold is the basic colour in this dish, so that the colour of the chicken comes out even better.

Nourishment for the mind

We eat and drink from physical necessity, and at the same time we want to eat food that is easily digested and as healthy as possible, preferably with as little fat and sugar as possible. In addition there is in eating a psychological need associated with a predictable pattern, nourished by our senses: smell, structure, temperature, sound and appearance. In Pastorale we want to give extra stimulation to this by playing on youthful memories, surprises, provocations and humour. An example will make this clear. An apple makes us think of specific predictable phenomena. It brings to mind a sweet smell, a specific red or green colour, a crunchy noise when we bite into it, and a sweet or sour taste. In Restaurant Pastorale we go a step further and we make sure that the apple we serve has all these predictable qualities to the extent that that apple makes you think of the orchard where you picked apples as a child. The surprise we create is, for instance, by serving a Tarte Tatin that doesn't look at all like a Tarte Tatin, but tastes just like one.

Arrangement of the book

This book begins where most others stop.
Beside every photograph is the name of the dish accompanied by a keyword which tries to sum up the essence of it.
Instead of setting out the recipe it is followed by a description of the sensations which the preparation produces
in the senses. In this way, apart from, obviously, the taste, the visual, aromatic and tactile values are also discussed.

Cock pheasant
Corn, grains, black salsify

104 **COHESION** This composition will recall impressions of outdoor life by using elements which are closely linked with each other. The cock pheasant's leg has been preserved and the breast has been roasted. This is accompanied by tasty crisps, of which the bird itself was also fond. The golden glow on the plate is a playful reference to the golden pheasant.

At the back of the book are the recipes of a number of elements in our preparations.
The intention is not that you should copy these dishes, but that the elements of them will inspire you to be creative.

name	ingredients	quantity	sequence	preparation	page
golden biscuit **based on polenta**	stock	1000 ml	1	Make a good stock and add the turmeric and the saffron to it. Bring to the boil.	104
	turmeric powder	6 g			
	saffron powder	1 g			
	polenta	100 g	2	Add the polenta and cook it until done. Add the guar gum and mix well.	
	guar gum	6 g			
			3	Spread the mixture thinly on a Sil-Pad. Leave to dry at 60°C.	

Baguette
chickpea puree and sesame seeds

CRUNCHY   Ingredients and taste carriers of hummus form the basis of this earthy and smooth snack. Traditionally Mediterranean in character, its structure and form give it a light crunchy and therefore contemporary appeal.

Sourdough bread

NATURE Made of dark multigrain flour which has been milled by natural stone and enriched with natural yeast from sour dough, we select sourdough bread as the most natural and authentic bread partner at table.

Parmesan soufflé

BAKED AIR With simple ingredients such as rice and parmesan we make a playful mouthful which we like to think of as 'baked air'. Crisp, airy and full of flavour, this technical tour de force produces a great deal of pleasure.

Bonbon of asparagus
Nutmeg and pesto of rocket

INTENSE We have tried to sum up in a single bite the finesse of one of the most complex and intense-tasting vegetables as subtly and yet forcefully as possible. To give the exceptional texture of this elegant delicacy a chance too, we arrange a soft flan next to the asparagus tip. Nutmeg and a pesto of rocket will provide extra expression and length of taste.

Gin & Tonic 2007

INSPIRATION For some compositions we find inspiration in classic cocktails. So a gin and tonic gave us the idea of combining the various structures of gin, apple and celery into a fresh and stimulating whole.

Tartare of forgotten varieties of tomatoes
Ricotta puree and mackerel

MILDLY SOUR   With these rich-tasting, old varieties of tomatoes we want in the first place to let people taste the complex and varied character of tomatoes as such. The fusion of tastes of fruit and vinegar provides new scope for their individuality and typical freshness in this dish. Ricotta puree provides a soft and refreshing sensation in the mouth, while its preparation with mackerel gives it an individual but very recognizable bite.

Marinated and impregnated tuna
Winter radish and mascarpone

IMPREGNATION Because of its meaty structure tuna lends itself perfectly for a number of creative preparations. Raw wrapped in nori, marinated, and impregnated with soya bouillon we get three different tuna tastes. Again with the winter radish we are looking for different shades of taste from the same basic ingredient. The salty cream of mascarpone and oysters offers a mild bridge between the dominant tuna and the two sharp-tasting radishes.

Oyster with a paste of horseradish,
soya jelly and pepper bread

HOT Some oysters are taste bombs, with a 'umami' nature which we want to make still stronger by, for instance, the use of strong soya jelly. Pepper bread, a hot, sharp paste of horseradish and a crisp salad of different varieties of radish provide extra savoury accents.

Poached venus shells and clams
Green algae, galangal and white roses

FLORAL Briefly poached shellfish, such as venus shells and clams, make for a mouth-watering, fluid texture and delicate, salty taste. A puree of algae reinforces the maritime character of this composition. Galangal root in combination with the perfume of white roses provides a floral dimension.

Raw langoustines,
structures of cauliflower and bulgur

SMOOTH Very fresh langoustines, removed from their shells, taste sweet, salty, smooth and creamy. Combining raw shellfish with cauliflower may seem unusual at first sight, but by using different structures, (crushed ice, cauliflower shredded raw or as a puree) and with bulgur cooked al dente with lime and star anise, you will produce refreshing sensations which will reinforce each other and leave lingering memories.

North Sea crab with algae and cream of algae

SALTY For this composition, complex in its appearance and structure, we have only used two ingredients. Algae are rich in pure, salty taste components, which are the perfect context for the soft, sweet flesh of the North Sea crab. Finished as a salad, jelly, cream and a biscuit, they bring out the various textures as well as the flavours in this dish.

Slow-cooked mackerel
Three ways with fennel

PRODUCT Young mackerel is a tasty illustration of our approach, in which each product, depending on the process it undergoes in the kitchen, can be interesting. To preserve its typical structure and rich taste, we cook the fish at a low temperature. To add to its presentation we work with the mild aniseed taste of fennel, which we introduce in three different ways. By combining it as a mousse, ice and crumble in the same mouthful with the fine structure of the fish, we experience an explosion of texture and temperature sensations.

Crisp-fried scallops
White cabbage, green apple, coriander and lime blossom

FRIVOLOUS Scallops should be crisp, juicy and at the same time silky-soft when they are served. By presenting each scallop with thin, crisp slices of pre-fried bread, we accentuate this sense of expectation. Down-to-earth cabbage and a julienne of winter radish give this combination a touch of 'earth and sea' allure. Mildly sour elements, such as Granny Smith apples, ginger and lime, give depth to the taste. An additional refreshing touch is given by the use of coriander and lime blossom.

Lukewarm oyster
Pumpkin puree, orange, mandarin and yuzu

CONTRAST Oysters cooked at a low temperature have a full, soft taste. Citrus fruits in various forms and textures offer salty, acidic and mildly sour contrasts. The pumpkin puree has been assembled with this in mind.

Raw and fried langoustines
Lasagne of carrots, with orange, ginger and cumin

COLOURFUL Sunny orange is the visual starting point of this composition, in which raw and briefly fried langoustines are the basis of a salty-sweet, hot-cold and texture-rich play of contrasts. Both grated carrot and carrot lasagne enrich this fascinating dish. Subtle use of preserved orange and ginger give it extra depth. As an additional liquid stimulant we serve a cocktail of carrot and ginger with it – but you can find out more about this on the next page.

Cocktail of carrot and ginger

AIRY This cocktail will supplement the two langoustine dishes of the previous page. With a fine-grained carrot granité and light and airy ginger foam we are still in the same atmosphere as far as taste, colour and texture is concerned. It is a supplementary composition, served in a separate glass, which accentuates the stimulation of this complex but harmonious dish in a liquid form.

Gently cooked haddock
Venus shell, lotus root and lime

MINERAL Haddock is an unfairly underrated fish in the restaurant world. It is tasty and firm in structure and is particularly juicy, and it is a pleasure to work with. This fish lends itself particularly well to very diverse combinations. Here we use apple and lime, because of their mild and aromatic acids. Lotus root, cucumber and turnips together add a surprising, mineral touch.

Marinated and gently cooked sea bass
Chicory and endive

MILDLY BITTER The texture of the velvety-soft sea bass is accentuated by briefly marinating it and allowing it to cook gently in a warm-water bath (Roner) until it reaches perfection. The mildly bitter tastes of chicory and endive give the dish an earthy and contrasting character.

Fried bass
Leeks, rhubarb and coconut

MOUTH SENSATIONS   An amusing exercise in taste is given by combining a number of typical products of our region with exotic ingredients. To bring out the delicate taste and structure of bass at its best, we fry the fillet on its skin. Only lime is used to enhance the natural taste. Leek puree with coconut as well as leek with rhubarb provide fine bitter-sweet touches. Leeks fried until crisp and coconut sponge cake are added for extra piquancy and for a pleasant sensation in the mouth.

Braised sole
Oyster, fresh lactic acids and cucumber

DAIRY PRODUCTS The fine taste and characteristic structure of sole is maintained by cooking the fish at a low temperature. An additional taste component is provided by 'Perle Blanche' oysters; their salty and mineral taste is enhanced by a cocktail of fresh acids. Yoghurt and buttermilk in various forms are its main companions, while cucumber, too, provides extra vegetable touches in various ways.

Turbot grilled on one side
Green paprika and green melon

REFRESHING The unique taste and juiciness of turbot responds perfectly to grilling. Reinforced by pepper and mint, the fish acquires an extra fresh dimension which we can enhance with restrained, playful garnishes based on paprika and melon.

Gilthead bream cooked slowly with dried fennel
Toasted aniseed spices with langoustine

TOASTING Mild spiciness, which should support the delicate meat of gilthead bream and certainly not dominate it, forms the starting point of this recipe. Fennel adds an aromatic character to the dish in various ways. Langoustines contribute an extra natural dimension of taste. This delicate shellfish always guarantees the addition of salty-sweet touches and extreme, almost liquid juiciness. Green tastes of fennel, Granny Smith apples and green olives provide an elegant link in this composition.

Fried ray and oyster
Cauliflower and couscous

SENSUAL Fried ray and oyster produce a silken and sensual sensation in the mouth which is reinforced by seaweed and oyster tartare in jelly. Fine-grained couscous with, for instance, capers and slivers of raw cauliflower, play their own part in that special feel in the mouth.

Slowly cooked eel from the East Scheldt
Purple artichokes and black olives

TERROIR The wonderful and delicate taste of the wild eel from the East Scheldt is unequalled. With the use of the Roner we coax perfection of taste and texture from one of my favourite products. This eel can be combined with an unending variety of tastes. For this recipe we opted for the bitter and full flavours of ingredients such as artichokes and black olives. The first we have used as it comes, as a puree and in a vinaigrette, while the olives are added as a crumble, in liquid form and in a crusty olive bread.

Fried gar
Purple artichokes and green olives

IN SEASON Gar, garpike or needlefish is not exactly a fish you will find on many menus. Nevertheless there are not many fish that can be served at the table in such a tasty way. Dismiss the thought of those awkward bones and gar would soon be as popular as sole or cod. Every year in May we serve a completely boneless preparation of gar. In this recipe this often scorned delicacy is accompanied by purple artichokes and green olives in various combinations. Two versatile products which will support the typical taste of this fish perfectly.

Fried scallops with hop shoots, oatmeal,
roasted parsley root and a cereal risotto

A NEW START The first hop shoots herald a new cycle of seasons. They taste fresh and fragile and can easily stand the power of, for instance, the last products of winter. We finish them off with a dash of wheat beer as a sour-bitter contrast to the delicate sweet taste of the scallops and the parsley root.

Crispy scallops
Belly of Berkshire pork, haricot beans, chorizo

CRISP   The basis of this dish is a traditional Italian bean soup. We retain the same rustic heartiness, but the crisply baked scallops are the central ingredient. Haricot beans are served in various pleasant structures. The chorizo sausage is worked into a biscuit, which with the aid of some oil makes a crisp and savoury garnish.

Red mullet cooked in olive oil
Forest mushrooms, celery and beer

IMPRESSION Oak stands at the centre in this dish, as in a forest walk, in which fallen oak leaves and ceps are the main ingredients. Maritime and earthy components united offer a fascinating challenge. Other ingredients, used in less obvious ways, such as beer crumbs and celery jelly, evoke a picture of a stimulating forest scene.

Marinated monkfish
Confit of pig's cheek, squid and puffed rice

JUICY The striking juiciness of monkfish comes out even better when a warm-water bath or Roner is used. And afterwards the bacon sees to it that this juiciness stays intact during baking. A confit of pig's cheek gives body to this dish. To add a Mediterranean touch we use preserved lemon and a pesto of black olives. Puffed rice adds another pleasant, crunchy detail to the dish.

Turnips and cauliflower
as a disk, crumbs, mayonnaise, roses, puree, cake and foam

STRUCTURES By offering a few vegetables in various structures, we can, with only a few ingredients, produce a fascinating, variegated dish with intense tastes. You can use these ingredients individually as supporting garnishes or offer them all on one plate as a whole spectrum of tastes and textures.

Roast Anjou pigeon
Red beetroot, cherries and horseradish

PURE To accompany the typically delicate taste of young Anjou pigeons we opt for restrained, mildly sour and delicate, piquant touches. Pure flavours of red beetroot, cherries and horseradish intentionally reinforce the same effect.

Roast wild duck
A quartet of chicory and cranberry structures

COMPLEXITY Wild duck is one of the first to proclaim the opening of the shooting and the chicory season, so we have combined the mildly bitter and tender meat with chicory, served in four different ways. A cranberry compote and jelly in their turn add mild, agreeable bitter notes to this composition.

Fried Barbary duck and goose liver
Impressions of cherries

TENSION Instead of the traditional cherries as the obvious accompaniment for duck, we have opted for a more acidic alternative in this recipe. Fresh morello cherries and cherry beer add more excitement and tension. The pleasant, sweet and playful accent has been retained by means of caramel with bitter chocolate. A little fried goose liver and a simple salad of radishes make sure of mouth-filling and refreshing accents.

Grilled hare from the polders
Puree and pralines of red beet and Jerusalem artichoke

EARTHY Hare from our polders is one of my favourite products to work with. As a purely natural product it is always a challenge to serve the rich-tasting meat on the plate at its best. By grilling we get the greatest benefit of the spiciness of the meat. The earthy flavours of the red beetroot and the Jerusalem artichoke are a fitting accompaniment.

Cock pheasant
Corn, grains, black salsify

COHESION This composition will recall impressions of outdoor life by using elements which are closely linked with each other. The cock pheasant's leg has been preserved and the breast has been roasted. This is accompanied by tasty crops, of which the bird itself was also fond. The golden glow on the plate is a playful reference to the golden pheasant.

Pauillac lamb with morels

HARBINGERS OF SPRING   In an early spring landscape, where the first green shoots have still to reveal themselves, we bring two typical spring products together. With crusty, butter-soft lamb and tender morels we serve a puree of celeriac, buckwheat cooked in lamb's gravy, and to provide a crisp touch, toasted buckwheat, and toasted millet and quinoa.

Fried goose liver
Pineapple, yuzu and liquorice

TEMPTING The exclusive and recognizable taste and structure of goose liver is given an extra dimension by smoking the liver very briefly. Exotic fruit, such as pineapple and yuzu used in various ways, give the whole a complex and tempting taste. Liquorice adds a striking detail.

Iced parfait of goat's cheese
Artichoke and white celery

SPICY The refreshing parfait of goat's cheese only has a crust of ice, so that the whole dish will melt away easily and gently. Fermented curry spices add spiciness which makes the goat's cheese even more attractive. We also use Vadouvan (curry mixture) in the artichoke gravy. Celery adds a fresh touch to balance the food.

Mandarin crumbs with yuzu

GLACIAL Ice structures made with liquid nitrogen at -196°C not only appeal to the imagination but also provide unknown sensations in the mouth. We use the delicate and aromatic acidity of mandarins and yuzu, which guarantee intensely scented pleasure.

Muscat melon
Orange, mango and vanilla

SCINTILLATING While playing with vegetables, fruit and spices you get a scintillating cocktail of harmonious and pure tastes on a plate. Refreshing as a snack, soothing after a cheese course or as preparation for a dessert in which, for instance, chocolate will demand all attention.

Mandarin
'Speculaas' and almonds

PLAYFUL More than with other courses, when we choose a dessert we like to opt for a creative, even playful element. Desserts indicate a finish to the meal. The serious work is done, it is time for a lighter touch. Here there is a faint reference to St Nicholas: 'speculaas' and mandarins. In these regions speculaas is a traditional spiced ginger biscuit, which is made in various shapes and sizes, and is one of the most popular treats the good Saint brings over from Spain each year.

Apricot cake

PLEASURE   Don't let us forget that eating well is in the first place a pleasant occupation. Desserts are extremely suitable to underline this. A frivolous creation around apricots satisfies this requirement and provides colour, taste and form for a sense of pleasure.

Pistachio structures

'JUST A LITTLE BIT NUTS' With a variation of structures we combine pistachio nuts with creamy nougat ice. You have to be 'a little bit nuts' to do this, but the effect proves that the efforts are worthwhile. Finished as a sauce, compote, cream, or grated, we taste the pistachio nuts, and it is quite different from the traditional pistachio ice cream.

Structures of coconut and banana

VERSATILE An amusing and tasty exercise to show how we can create a rich spectrum of possibilities with just a few ingredients. In tropical countries coconuts are used for a variety of things. They are just as versatile in the kitchen. And here we have just been inspired by Batida de Coco, a cocktail of a Brazilian liqueur with coconut milk.

Rhubarb combined with Mara strawberries

SCENTED Young rhubarb is a delicious product with a complex taste, which develops special depths according to the way it is prepared. Combined with the scent of aromatic Mara strawberries we discover fascinating and complementary sensations on our plate.

Blueberries
Tart, foam, juice, granité, marshmallow

FEMININE With this recipe we bring you our own interpretation of a classic blueberry tart. With respect for tradition and as a 'clue' we serve a piece of it with associated structures beside it, such as a coulis, granité, foam and marshmallows. The dish is completed by a yoghurt ice.

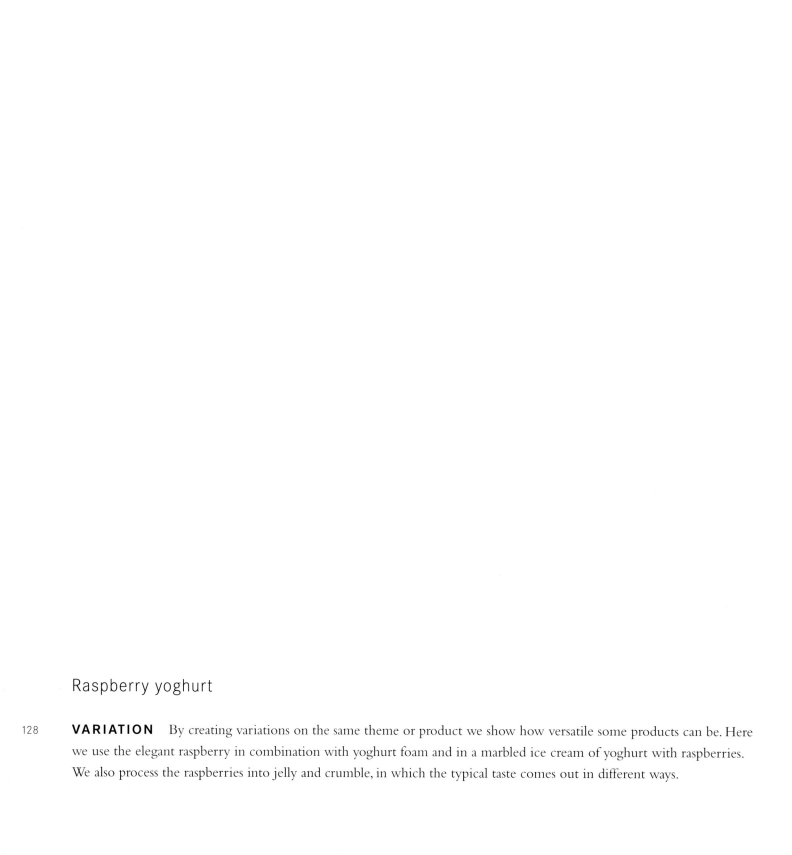

Raspberry yoghurt

VARIATION By creating variations on the same theme or product we show how versatile some products can be. Here we use the elegant raspberry in combination with yoghurt foam and in a marbled ice cream of yoghurt with raspberries. We also process the raspberries into jelly and crumble, in which the typical taste comes out in different ways.

Pinky pinky, or sweet impressions of pink
Raspberry, cassis

AMUSING We don't leave people with a really sweet tooth out in the cold, but they will have to wait until the end of the feast. Once all other taste impressions have had their way, we give our full attention to the final sweets. Both aromatic fruit, soft, melting ice cream, sweets from grandmother's days or carnival specialities such as spun sugar, will cater for a childish accent at the end of a festive meal.

**Three times figs,
twice white chocolate**

FLUID To convert figs into a preserve and even a coulis gives this pre-eminently crunchy fruit a special fluid dimension. White chocolate made into a paste and ice cream provide a smooth consistency, while *wentelteefjes*, a local version of French toast, finish off this dessert.

Apple tart, version 2007

CRUMBS For a contemporary apple dessert we focus on crisp crumbs for this interpretation of the traditional Tarte Tatin. Not only apples, but nuts, lemons and spices are highly suitable for this. The traditional scoop of vanilla ice cream is the ideal and melting link between all these multifarious ingredients.

Almonds

AROMATIC Sugared almonds are always very popular, but almonds used in pannacotta, macaroons and almond paste also release their aroma freely. Here we combine the obvious with the surprising. In this dish we combine recognizable, crisp almond slivers with a spaghetti based on almond tea.

Choc-o-'Valrhona'

ENDLESS Chocolate is one of those rare products with which you can experiment almost endlessly in the kitchen. This preparation is the result of a great deal of preparatory fiddling which in the end sorts out the complexity of various Valrhona specialities. A joy for chocoholics, but 'ordinary' fans will also be stunned to discover how the rich chocolate can taste.

Nespresso lolly

DEPTH We have opted for Nespresso as a 'house' coffee, because this assortment has been specially developed for restaurants and is richly variegated. In its range of tastes each variety has unimaginable depth and their seasonal collections are always a pleasant addition to the standard palette of flavours. Here this same coffee forms the basis for a frivolous dessert in which chocolate provides the supplementary body.

Boudoirs and tonka

FRAGILE Boudoir biscuits or sponge fingers are a classic in the patisserie kitchen. In this recipe we accentuate the fragile, light and crisp character of the biscuits by coating both sides with a lovely, crisp layer of sugar.

Macaroons of star anise

CLASSIC Macaroons are more popular than ever and the adaptations appear to be endless. Here we have deliberately opted for a visually simple application, which enhances the exotic scent of the fragrant star anise even more.

Pralines of chocolate,
olive and preserved tomatoes

PIQUANT This praline, made of pure chocolate, is given a very special twist. Sweetness and piquancy are elegantly interwoven. In addition we create a smooth and crunchy feel in the mouth.

Deep-fried ice lolly

CONTRASTS Looking for extremes in the kitchen we first make a lemon foam solid in liquid nitrogen (–196 °C) before frying it in sugar. The result is a stimulating lolly with a crisp outer skin covering a smooth, refreshing mousse.

The sixth sense: emotion

'With sensory sensations we create emotions, the sixth sense. To activate that sixth sense we have a spectrum of products and techniques in the kitchen which – dependent on what we use or how we apply them – can bring about small or strong emotions. That is also possible by taking something out of its normal context, or by creating an unexpected association which, for instance, may call up memories from a distant past. An amusing detail on the plate, a culinary provocation, a surprising effect, a new texture, an unusual concentration of tastes, a peculiar appearance, or tingling and refreshing tartness…
We are continually looking for possible ways of making and creating tastes to surprise our guests and to make them experience something special. It is how we communicate. Letting people taste something which makes them look at each other, then to try it again and relax while chatting, wondering precisely what they have experienced. That is our ambition. That is what we are here for. Day after day.'

Chris Gordon Somkit

Chris is the silent power in the kitchen, rarely heard but always at the ready. He is a perfectionist, very strong on the technicalities of taste, and he oversees every detail. His wide knowledge of products and tastes forms the basis of his work, which is always at a very high level. He is concerned with taste and has particularly mastered the finesse of sweet–and–sour combinations. Chris moves mountains of work and focuses particularly on the preparation of hot vegetable dishes. That he does so in a calm, almost serene manner is an extra bonus for the kitchen. He has revealed himself to be a real workhorse with vision and has already been part of our team for four years.

Pieter Van Dessel   Marie-Claire Braem

Pieter joined us last year. He is to me the prototype of the inquisitive staff member and spontaneous applicant, who continually wants to appease his hunger for knowledge and so came to Pastorale. Driven to acquire a knowledge of products and technical know-how, he worked himself up in a very short time to be a very good taster, and hence became a very efficient colleague. He is responsible for patisserie and the treats that accompany coffee or tea. It is no surprise that Pieter has a particularly sweet tooth!

My wife always has a listening ear within the team. Marie-Claire was trained as a social worker and at first also worked in that sector. Her knowledge and experience serve her well in Pastorale. She has had to deal with a great many problems in those years, so that she has been seasoned in her job. Marie-Claire carries out everything very efficiently and as requested, but often still does her own thing if it is in everyone's interest. I like to compare her to a dish that you can still hear sizzling when it is being served, and so arouses extra interest and attention.

Jon Stalmans

Jon has been responsible for building up our wine cellar for more than ten years. That he shares my preference for wines from Germany, Italy and Spain is a bonus for our cooperation. His preference for wines with fresh and elegant acidity will therefore not arouse any surprise. Jon, of course, has a very well-developed nose. He can recognize very many wines just by their aroma and their bouquet. He can also call on a richly developed taste palette and a highly developed ability to recognize wines, which makes him an expert at blind tastings. Jon classes his wines solely on the basis of their taste. As he is very finicky, he makes sure that even the smallest details are given proper attention. That he then sometimes pulls me by the sleeve, I can only appreciate. And with his elephantine memory I also consider him to be the collective memory bank of our restaurant.

Jan Bleys   Bart De Pooter

Art historian, urbanist and garden designer: I came to know Jan Bleys twelve years ago as an extremely versatile professional. Jan is the external designer with an indispensable touch in our team. I appreciate his great feeling for homogeneous, pure and harmonious spaces. He has stimulated my spatial thinking and feel for design. Jan gave our entire premises an overall form, in which much attention was paid to the authentic splendour and to the origin of the building. Both the interior and the surroundings, particularly the garden, were formed by him into a conceptual and intensely tangible unity.

Fifteen years ago Pastorale was already a robust, healthy baby and meanwhile it has grown up into a sturdy adolescent. Throughout this time I have attempted to get the best out of my staff and myself. My efforts to share my convictions with them, so that they in turn can convey them to our guests, come first. To make myself clear, I call this point of view the philosophy of Pastorale. Our aim is not only to stimulate the five best-known senses, but also the emotions of our guests. With a wink and a sense of humour, an element of surprise, or by taking something out of context, we try to activate their sixth sense too. It seems to me that if we can also stimulate and play on the emotions, then we are well on the way to achieving our mission successfully.

Index

In the index are a number of preparations which form part of a dish.
They are classified by their structure.
The recipes are intended to be a source of inspiration for the development of new dishes and to assist/support creativity.

name	ingredients	quantity	sequence	preparation	page

crisp & crunchy, caramels and other dishes

name	ingredients	quantity	sequence	preparation	page
migas of pistachio nuts	bread without crusts		1	Crumble the bread, but neither too fine, not too coarse.	120
	peanut oil		2	Deep-fry the bread at 170°C. Leave to drain well on paper.	
	pistachio praline pistachio nuts, roasted		3	Mix the deep-fried bread with some praline and roasted pistachio nuts.	
apricot biscuit with isomalt	apricot puree	150 g		Mix everything together at 80°C in the Thermomix until you have a nice smooth mixture. Spread onto a mould and bake for 35 minutes at 110°C. Roll the baked biscuit round a rod into a tube. Keep in a dry place.	118
	soft white sugar	20 g			
	isomalt	25 g			
	glucose	5 g			
algae biscuit	tapioca flour	200 g	1	Cook the tapioca flower with the algal water to a glassy mixture.	56
	algae powder	30 g	2	Add the algae powder.	
	algal water	1000 ml			
			3	Smooth the mixture thinly on greaseproof paper and dry for 1 hour at 120°C.	
rice crackers	rice	50 g		Add everything together, bring to the boil and steam gently, so that the rice grains stay whole. Pack the mass in foil and leave to solidify in the freezer. Cut this into very thin slices with a cutter. Dry them in an Easydry for 24 hours at 50°C. Deep-fry them in oil at 200°C.	92
	water	100 ml			
	ink from squid	20 ml			
	salt	1 g			
bitter chocolate crumbs	flour	120 g	1	Mix everything together.	100
	butter	100 g	2	Shape into a block and put into the freezer.	
	cocoa	20 g			
	brown sugar	10 g	3	Grate onto a baking tray using a Microplane grater. Bake in the oven at 120°C.	
	coarse salt	10 g			
	malt	20 g			
raspberry crumbs	flour	300 g	1	Mix everything together.	128
	raspberries, dried	100 g	2	Leave it to set.	
	sugar	250 g			
	butter, melted	250 g	3	Grate it finely and bake in the oven at 120°C.	
crisp biscuit of vegetable puree, malt, guar gum	flour	100 g	mass A	Mix the flour, the malt and the butter.	76
	malt	50 g			
	butter	50 g			
	vegetable puree	100 g	mass B		

name	ingredients	quantity	sequence	preparation	page
	stock	20 ml		Refresh the thick vegetable puree with raw and partly reduced stock.	
	guar gum	1 g		Add the guar gum and allow to stand for 12 hours.	
	application:				
	mass A	50 g		Spread thinly onto a tray.	
	mass B	30 g		Bake it in the oven for 8 minutes at 100°C.	
grains of lamb gravy	dried mushrooms	50 g		Boil everything together for 40 minutes, until the rice is well done.	106
	mineral water	1250 ml		Mix it all in the Thermomix and strain it.	
	lamb gravy	1000 ml		Smooth the paste out onto a baking paper and leave to dry in the oven for 3 hours at 90°C or overnight at 60°C.	
	soya sauce	250 ml			
	rice, bomba	500 g		Leave for one day out of the oven and then keep it in an open container. Grind it, but not too fine. Deep-fry it in separate portions in hot oil at 180°C.	
breadcrumbs, salty (use: frying oysters)	panko (Japanese dried breadcrumbs)	100 g		Grind finely in the Thermomix.	74
	rice flour	10 g			
	algae powder	10 g			
	green tea powder	10 g			
	oysters, e.g. perles blanches	12		Coat oysters on one side and fry them crisp in olive oil.	
	olive oil				
golden biscuit based on polenta	stock	1000 ml	1	Make a good stock and add the turmeric and the saffron to it. Bring to the boil.	104
	turmeric powder	6 g			
	saffron powder	1 g			
	polenta	100 g	2	Add the polenta and cook it until done. Add the guar gum and mix well.	
	guar gum	6 g			
			3	Spread the mixture thinly on a Sil-Pad. Leave to dry at 60°C.	
waffle batter	butter	200 g	1	Make the milk lukewarm.	90
	milk	250 ml		Dissolve the yeast and the butter.	
	Duvel beer	250 ml		Add the Duvel.	
	yeast	35 g		Fold in the flour.	
	flour	500 g		Add the salt.	
	salt	5 g			
	mushroom powder	150 g			
			2	Spread the batter thinly onto a Sil-Pad and bake it in the oven.	

Optional: distillation of young oak root. This makes a crisp biscuit with touches of yeast.
It is, for instance an ideal way to suggest a wood in autumn.

name	ingredients	quantity	sequence	preparation	page

juices, infusions, stocks, sauces

name	ingredients	quantity	sequence	preparation	page
galangal base	pears, peeled and cut small	3	1	Put all ingredients together in a pan and just cover with water. Simmer for 40 minutes without letting it come to boiling point. Leave it to drain in a muslin cloth.	52
	galangal	1 root			
	lemon grass	1 stalk			
	lemon zest	10 g			
galangal jelly	galangal base	320 ml		Heat the galangal base with the agar-agar to 80°C. Allow to cool to 40°C and then add the pre-soaked gelatine. Pour onto a tray and leave to set.	52
	agar-agar	1 g			
	gelatine	2 g			
galangal vinaigrette	galangal base	200 g		Add all ingredients to the cold galangal base and heat to 80°C. Allow it to cool again to a floppy jelly.	52
	galangal, grated	10 g			
	lemon peel, grated	10 g			
	lemon juice	20 ml			
	eel pout	1 g			
pesto of black olives	black olives, pitted	100 g		Add everything together and mix to a smooth mass. Bring to taste and put through a fine sieve. Keep in a closed container.	92
	anchovy	20 g			
	garlic, roasted	20 g			
	olive oil	50 ml			
	cayenne pepper				
	lemon, preserved and juice	5 g			
	squid ink	25 ml			
	xantana	1 g			
carrot vinaigrette	carrot juice, made with a Greenstar juicer	1000 ml	1	Add all these ingredients together.	108
	orange juice	400 ml			
	yuzu vinegar	100 ml			
	sugared water	200 ml			
	salt	10 g			
	tara gum	6.8 g	2	Bind the mixture with tara gum.	
	olive oil	560 g	3	Add the olive oil.	

name	ingredients	quantity	sequence	preparation	page
fennel syrup	vinegar	100 ml	1	Mix all ingredients of 1 and reduce to caramel.	76
	sugar	100 g			
	Ricard	100 ml			
	star anise	2			
	fennel	5000 g	2	Process the fennel in a juicer and boil to reduce.	
			3	Add the fennel liquid to the caramel. Let it boil into a syrup.	
			4	Strain the syrup through a fine sieve and keep it in a sauce bottle.	
soya marinade	Nilgiri tea	450 ml		Make a strong Nilgiri tea.	48
	soya	90 g		Add 10 g crushed black penja pepper and strain the tea at once.	
	pepper	10 g		Bring to taste with soya.	
mayonnaise **of apple and lime blossom** (use: warm mayonnaise with metil as a gellifier)	*juices*				60
	Granny Smith	5		Press the Granny Smiths in a juicer and add the lime juice.	
	limes	4			
	preparation				
	juice	400 ml	1	Bring the lime-blossom tea to the boil with the agar-agar and the carragheen gum.	
	lime blossom tea	100 ml	2	Leave to cool and add the juice.	
	carragheen gum	1.5 g	3	Put the mixture together with the metil in the Thermomix.	
	agar-agar	2 g	4	Next put it in a syphon and use two gas cartridges.	
	metil	4 g			

name	ingredients	quantity	sequence	preparation	page

foam, mousse, bavarois (cold), espumas

name	ingredients	quantity	sequence	preparation	page
bombe glacée **based on gelatine and metil**	liquid gelatine liquid metil	500 ml 10 g 100 ml 3 g	1 2	25°C 3°C Whisk 1 briskly. Next add 2. Fill deep-freeze mats and put them in the freezer.	44
tonic bombe	fennel bouillon apple juice with lime tonic water gelatine grapefruit juice lime juice metil	150 ml 100 ml 150 ml 10 g 80 ml 20 ml 3 g	1 2 3	Heat the fennel bouillon to 40°C. Dissolve the gelatine in it. Pour the apple juice and lime together with the tonic water into the bouillon. Leave to cool until the gelatine is beginning to set. Mix and dissolve. Allow to cool to 3°C or cooler. Whisk 1 in a Kenwood mixer to a foaming mass. Add mixture 2 to mixture 1. Whisk everything together Pipe into moulds and fast-freeze until set.	44
asparagus bonbon	asparagus puree agar-agar gelatine cream clarified butter with tarragon vinegar vegetarian gelatine (Sosa) cream	800 g 5 g 4 leaves 200 ml 500 ml 15 g 50 ml	1 2 3 4 5 .	Mix the cold asparagus puree with the agar-agar and heat up to 80°C. Leave to cool. Add the gelatine at 40°C. Leave to cool more and at 20°C add the partly whipped cream. Fill mats with half rounds and leave to set in the refrigerator. Mix the clarified butter with the gelatine and heat up to 70°C. Lower the temperature to 40°C and pass the bonbon through the mixture. Arrange straight onto a spoon and finish off with asparagus and pesto.	42

name	ingredients	quantity	sequence	preparation	page
ginger foam	syrup of preserved ginger	200 ml	1	Infuse the syrup and pass it through a strainer. Add the pre-soaked gelatine.	66
	cumin	10 g			
	gelatine	8 g			
	buttermilk	250 ml	2	Mix the buttermilk with the lemon juice and bind this while cold with xantana in the Thermomix. Turn for 5 minutes.	
	lemon juice	50 ml			
	xantana	1.5 g			
			3	Add 1 and 2 together. Put in a syphon. Use one gas cylinder.	
espuma of gin & tonic	tonic water	400 ml	1	Use Thermomix for mixing, first tonic, gin and citras.	44
	gin	100 ml	2	Bind this with the xantana.	
	xantana	1.5 g	3	Heat this mixture to 40°C.	
	citras	2 g	4	Add the soaked gelatine.	
	gelatine leaves	12 g	5	Put the mixture into an ice-cold espuma flask and leave to cool in iced water. Use two gas cylinders. Keep cold.	
espuma of yoghurt and buttermilk (use: high acidity espuma syphon)	yoghurt	350 ml	1	Mix the buttermilk with the xantana.	74
	buttermilk	150 ml	2	Add the albumen and mix well.	
	albumen (egg-white powder)	3 g	3	Add the yoghurt last.	
	xantana	2 g	4	Put the mixture into a syphon; use 2 gas cartridges.	

name	ingredients	quantity	sequence	preparation	page

ice cream, granitas, sorbets, crushed ice and other preparations

name	ingredients	quantity	sequence	preparation	page
granita of carrots	carrot juice	1000 ml	1	Bind the carrot juice cold with xantana.	66
	xantana	3 g			
	orange juice	400 ml	2	Bring the orange juice with the sugar to the boil.	
	yuzu vinaigrette	100 ml		Add the yuzu vinaigrette and allow to cool.	
	sugar	270 g			
	salt		3	Add 1 and 2 together and add salt to taste.	
			4	Leave to set in the deepfreeze.	
				Scrape off with a fork or with a mandoline.	
	This recipe can also be used for a juice.				
crushed fennel ice	fennel puree of fennel leaves and dill	220 g	1	Make fennel puree of only the green leaves of the fennel and dill.	58
	cream	150 ml	2	Mix the cooled down puree with the other ingredients in 2.	
	stock	100 ml			
	cooking liquid	100 ml			
	gelatine	3 g	3	Dissolve the gelatine and add it to the other ingredients.	
			4	Put this in 'Paco Jet' pots and keep it for 12 hours at -20°C.	
fennel ice	fennel puree, white	1500 g	1	Mix everything.	58
	cream	500 ml	2	Put the mixture in a vacuum pack and cook for 20 minutes at 83°C till done.	
	Ricard	100 ml	3	Cool quickly in iced water.	
	egg yolk	150 g	4	Fill a 'Paco Jet' pot and cool for 12 hours at -20°C.	
	lemon zest	20 g	5	Finish off by turning for as long as the quantity demands.	
	fennel syrup	100 ml			
celery and apple granita	apples	3 apples	1	Peel the apples and liquidize them: to avoid discolouring catch the juice in a jar with lime juice.	44
	lime juice	3 limes			
	celery, white	5 stalks		Put the celery through a Greenstar liquidizer and strain the juice.	
				Add the juices which have to acquire a taste of celery.	
	tara gum	5 g/l	2	Bind with 5 g tara gum per litre for a cold binding.	
			3	Freeze in an oblong container with a lid.	
			4	Scrape loose with a fork before use.	

name	ingredients	quantity	sequence	preparation	page

jelly preparations

morel jelly / gellan

base

					106
	shallots	50 g	1	Reduce to 100 ml.	
	madeira	150 ml			
	morel stock	250 ml	2	Add to 1 and bring to the boil.	
	consommé	150 ml		Strain and season to taste.	
	sherry vinegar	40 ml		Allow to cool.	
	thyme	5 g			

gellan

	base	500 ml	3	Bring the cold stock to the boil with the gellan.
	gellan	18 g		Leave to set into a block.
			4	Create fine strings by grating the block with a Microplane grater.

chocolate preparations

chocolate bonbon with sun-dried tomatoes and szechuan pepper

	sun-dried tomatoes	50 g	1	Bring these ingredients to the boil, infuse and strain.	146
	szechuan pepper, roasted	15 g			
	cream	800 ml			
	white chocolate	200 g	2	Join 1 and 2 together.	
	pure chocolate 811	800 g			
	olive oil	100 ml		Pour the mixture into a square mould.	
				Leave it to set. Cut it into small cubes.	
	Cover with tablet chocolate 811		3	Cover the cubes with chocolate 811.	

purees

leeks and rhubarb puree with coconut

coconut fond

					72
	coconut milk	1000 ml		Bring to the boil and infuse.	
	lemongrass	5			
	lemon peel	50 g			
	lemon juice	20 ml			

puree

	leeks	1000 g		Bring the coconut fond back to the boil.
	rhubarb	200 g		Add everything and cook till well done.
	coconut fond	1000 ml		Mix and strain.
	sugar	to taste		
				Reduce until the desired consistency had been reached.

name	ingredients	quantity	sequence	preparation	page
bread, cakes, etc.					
apricot cake	white chocolate	160 g	1	Melt the chocolate and the butter together.	118
	butter	125 g		Add the egg yolks one at the time.	
	egg yolk	75 g			
	fine brunoise of dried apricots	160 g	2	Add 2 to 1.	
	zest of orange	20 g			
	cardamom	5 g			
	egg white	130 g	3	Whisk egg whites and sugar to meringue consistency.	
	sugar	105 g		Add this to 1.	
	flour	65 g	4	Finally fold in the flour.	
			5	Bake for 10 minutes at 180°C.	
pistachio cake (microwave)	pistachio nuts	190 g	1	Grind the dry ingredients very fine in the Thermomix.	120
	green tea	25 g	2	Mix the oil with the egg yolk.	
	pasteurized egg whites	250 g	3	Next add the egg whites to the egg yolks.	
	egg yolks	160 g	4	Add all this to the dry ingredients in the Thermomix and let it run quickly.	
	flour	40 g		Don't allow the mixture to get warm.	
	sugar	165 g	5	Put the mixture into a syphon and use four gas cylinders.	
	olive oil	25 ml	6	Pipe the mixture into plastic beakers, filling them 1/3 full.	
			7	Put this in a 750 watt microwave for 50 seconds.	
			8	Leave to cool for 2 minutes.	
coconut sponge cake	coconut, fresh, ground	1000 g	1	Grind the fresh coconut.	72
	powdered egg white	100 g	2	Mix the powdered egg white with the buttermilk and whisk it.	
	buttermilk	600 ml			
			3	Fold 2 into 1. Pour the mixture onto a tray with mat and cling film.	
			4	Steam for 15 minutes at 90°C. Put it in the freezer to facilitate cutting.	
olive cake	eggs	10	1	Whisk the eggs with the olive oil till light and airy. Add 2. Fold 3 lightly into the mixture.	82
	olive oil	400 ml			
	salt	5 g	2	Bake for 20 minutes in the oven at 170°C.	
	lemon zest	20 g			
	lemon juice	40 ml			
	olives, green, brunoise	500 g			
	anchovy	60 g			
	flour	470 g	3		
	baking powder	15 g			

name	ingredients	quantity	sequence	preparation	page
olive bread	white flour	1000 g		Mix everything and knead for 20 minutes.	82
	rye	100 g		Leave to rest.	
	bran	100 g		Divide the dough into portions of 425 g.	
	salt	30 g		Put the portions in oiled moulds.	
	olive oil	150 ml		Leave the dough to rise for 40 minutes at 32°C.	
	water	600 ml		Bake the loaves for 40 minutes at 180°C.	
	yeast	50 g			
	pulp of black olives, mixed and strained through a fine sieve	500 g			
black nori bread	flour	1200 g	1		48
recipe for 4 loaves	nori powder	50 g	2	Make a black paste and add it to the flour.	
	buttermilk	500 ml			
	yoghurt	500 ml			
	cocoa	50 g			
	anchovies	100 g			
	garlic puree	20 g			
	cayenne	3 g			
	squid ink	100 ml			
	soya sauce	200 ml			
	butter	60 g	3	Add remaining ingredients.	
	yeast	60 g		Knead for 10 minutes.	
	bread improver	40 g			
				Leave the dough to rise.	
				Bake the bread.	

name	ingredients	quantity	sequence	preparation	page
preserves					
brunoise of green paprika, transparent preserve	water	1000 ml	1	Make sugared water with all ingredients of 1. Strain before use. Set aside ice-cold.	76
	sugar	500 g			
	lemon verbena	20 g			
	lemon grass	2 stalks			
	zest of two lemons				
	paprika	1	2	Peel the paprika. Cut it into a fine brunoise. Blanch this in boiling water. Cool immediately in the ice-cold sugared water.	
preserved lotus root	water	1000 ml	1	Prepare sugared water. Add all other ingredients, bring to the boil and leave to infuse. Strain the mixture.	68
	sugar	150 g			
	salt	20 g			
	lime juice	200 ml			
	galangal	100 g			
	zest of 5 limes				
	lotus root	1	2	Peel the lotus root. Use a cutter to cut it into thin slices.	
			3	Poach the slices in water. Drain them.	
			4	Add them to the sugared water. Bring to the boil. Leave it to cool and then it is ready for use.	
rice, cereals and pâté					
couscous (use: rye)	couscous	100 g	1	Steam the couscous until done in a stock of coriander and lime.	80
	capers	10 g	2	Finish off with capers, raw cauliflower, coriander, zest of lemon, lime juice and finely chopped algae.	
	cauliflower, raw	20 g			
	coriander	5 g			
	grated lemon	5 g			
	lime juice				
	algae, poached and finely chopped	10 g			

name	ingredients	quantity	sequence	preparation	page
biscuits					
boudoir	eggs	7	1	Whip into a foam.	142
	sugar	350 g			
	flour	400 g	2	Fold in the flour, the tonka and the baking powder.	
	tonka	20 g			
	baking powder	10 g			
			3	Pipe into silicon mat. Sprinkle with sugar. Bake for 11 minutes at 170°C.	
aniseed macaroons	eggs	250 g	1	Whisk the eggs with the soft sugar for 12 minutes at setting 4.	144
	soft white sugar	400 g			
	flour	400 g	2	Fold the flour into it.	
	aniseed powder	18 g			
			3	Pipe small rounds of the mixture.	
	sugar S2	75 g	4	Sprinkle sugar on the rounds.	
			5	Leave them to rest for three hours.	
			6	Bake for 12 minutes at 150°C, leaving the oven slightly open, so that moisture can escape.	

name	ingredients	quantity	sequence	preparation	page

inversas

name	ingredients	quantity	sequence	preparation	page
olive drops (inversa)	*basic sauce*				82
	black olives	500 g	1	Mix everything.	
	barigoule sauce	200 ml		Strain the mixture.	
	olive oil	100 ml			
	preserved lemon	1			
	walnut oil	50 ml			
	sauce drops				
	basic sauce	1000 ml	2	Process the gluco and liquid cold in the Thermomix.	
	gluco	20 g		Extract air by means of a vacuum pump.	
	algin bath				
	water (Spa reine)	1500 ml	3	Put a small spoonful of 2 in the algin bath.	
	alginate	7.5 g		Wait 2 minutes.	
				Rinse the drops with still water.	
				Keep them in olive oil.	
muscatel drops (inversa)	muscatel	500 ml	1	Stabilize the alcohol with the xantana.	134
	xantana	1 g		Add the gluco and let it turn well in the Thermomix.	
	gluco	4 g		Extract the air by means of a vacuum pump.	
	water (Spa reine)	1000 ml	2	Mix the water with the alginate.	
	alginate	5 g		Extract the air by means of a vacuum pump or leave to rest overnight.	
				Use the algin bath at room temperature.	
				Put a small spoonful of base I into the algin bath.	
				Leave to rest in it for 2.5 minutes.	
				Take it out and dip it into a bath of still water.	
				Keep it in muscatel.	

www.lannoo.com

Lannoo Publishers nv
Kasteelstraat 97 – B-8700 Tielt
lannoo@lannoo.be
De Wetstraat 1 – NL-6814 AN Arnhem
info@terralannoo.nl

Restaurant Pastorale
Bart De Pooter
Laarstraat 22
BE - 2840 Reet
Tel. + 32 3 844 65 29
Fax + 32 3 844 73 47
www.depastorale.be
pastorale@belgacom.net

Recipes: Bart De Pooter
Text: Willem Asaert
English translation: Alastair and Cora Weir
Photography: Bart Van Leuven
Photographic assistants: Tom Swijns and Lisa Van Damme
Graphic designer: Inge Van Damme

© Uitgeverij Lannoo nv, Tielt, 2008
D/2008/45/491 – NUR 440

ISBN: 978-90-209-8128-5

Printed and bound by Die Keure, Bruges, 2008

The publisher has made every effort to observe the author's rights to the poem as laid down by law. Anyone who in spite of this still believes to have rights to it should approach the publisher.

All rights reserved. No part of this book may be reproduced, stored in an automatic retrieval system and/or published in any form or by any means, electronic, mechanical or otherwise, without prior written permission of the publisher.